Karmann 4-seater Cabriolet and Hebmüller 2-seater Cabriolet introduced

Side ventilation flaps added to A-panels; Wolfsburg crest on export model

Engine capacity increased to 1192 cc (VW 1200)

Anti-roll bar added to front axle

One-piece oval window replaces split-window

Semaphore indicator arms eliminated

Windshield enlarged; rear window significantly enlarged

Glossy finish and chrome plating added

Export (US) Beetle introduced

1946 1947 1948 1949 1950 1951 1952 1953 1954 1955 1956 1957 1958 1959

Vent windows, 15-inch wheels added

Folding sunroof introduced; hydraulic brakes added to export

Type 51 (sedan body on Kübel chassis) produced; Type 11 engine increased from 985 cc to 1131 cc.

Concept 1, modeled after Beetle, presented at the North American International Auto Show in Detroit on January 5th, 1994

Last year for German-built Beetle sedan; production lasts into January 1978

Engine updated to fuel injection; Le Grande Bug (Sport Bug with sport wheels) introduced

Production of new Beetle started Fall 1997

Beetles continue to be produced in Mexico and Brazil throughout the '80s and '90s

1974 1975 1976 1977 1978 1979 1980   1994 1995 1996 1997 1998

New Beetle released March 1998

Energy-absorbing bumpers added

Super Beetle sedan discontinued

Production of Beetle Cabrio ceases in January 1980

Concept 1 convertible introduced at the New York Auto Show on March 29th, 1994

- Changes are referenced by model year
- Post-1949, only U.S. export models covered

Edwin Baaske

VOLKSWAGEN BEETLE

PORTRAIT OF A LEGEND

RB

ROBERT BENTLEY
AUTOMOTIVE PUBLISHERS

ТOMOTIVE PUBLISHERS

Information that makes
the difference.®

1734 Massachusetts Avenue
Cambridge, MA 02138 USA
800-423-4595 / 617-547-4170
http://www.rb.com
e-mail: sales@rb.com

Copies of this book may be purchased from selected booksellers,
or directly from the publisher by mail. Please write to Robert
Bentley, Inc., Publishers at the address listed on the top of this
page.

Library of Congress Cataloging-in-Publication Data
Baaske, Edwin.
    [VW Käfer. English]
    Volkswagen Beetle: portrait of a legend / Edwin Baaske.
        p.   cm.
    ISBN 0-8376-0162-2 (alk. paper): Robert Bentley
    ISBN 3-7688-0901-3: Delius Klasing
    1. Volkswagen automobile—Pictorial works. 2. Volkswagen
automobile—History. I. Title.
    TL215.V6B33   1997
    629.222'2—dc21   97-42149
                                                    CIP

Bentley Stock No. GVBE
01 00 99 98 10 9 8 7 6 5 4 3 2 1

Manufactured in Hong Kong

Photographs:

Toni Angermayer (1), Carl-Heinz Baaske (2),
Albert Breiteneicher (1), dpa (1), Gunter Hartmann/Maxima (1),
Andreas Beyer (1), Gute Fahrt Archiv (16), Siegfried Hartig (1),
Gunter Hartmann (2), Wolfgang Hocke (1), P.I. Hoffmann (1),
Hannes Kilian (2), Hans Joachim Klersy (9), Peter C. Kunert (1),
Presse Seeger (1), Matthias Meier (1), Dr. Ludwig Merkle (2),
Hermann Rest (1), Ulrich Schwab (1), Wolfgang Speckmann (1),
Hans Truöl (2), Volkswagen Archiv (84), Volkswagen of America (4),
Bernd Weiser (1), Julius Weitmann (1), Helmut Wildenhain (1),
Arthur Westrup (4)

Page Design: Klaus Killenberg

Translator: Erik S. Meyers

CONTENTS

Even now there are still 200,000 Beetles cruising Germany's roads. In the mid 60s, when roadways still meant tree-lined boulevards, practically every other car in Germany was a Volkswagen, the chief export of a relatively young republic.

Grandma Elisabeth's 80th birthday party was larger than any birthday celebration my family has had to date. There was much cake and praise for this cheerful, petite woman, who still has many fulfilling years ahead of her. Her presence and strength have kept my family together all these years—she has been a guiding force for all of us. To honor her and to remind ourselves how much she is a part of our lives, we put together a wonderful slide show. The images on the screen reflected our

TIME MACHINE

family history: uncles and aunts posing in front of split-window Beetles, men in army uniforms, streets of row houses: homes and horizons that have expanded over time. Many of the pictures seemed foreign to me but those in which Grandma Elisabeth appeared reminded me how important she is to our family. Those memories and thoughts on that special day in the spring of 1995 moved me to write this book.

Grandma Elisabeth is to her family what the Beetle is to those who truly appreciate it: an old, family member we rely upon, a symbol of times past. The Beetle is like a time machine that takes us all the way back to our parents' adolescence. The very existence of the Beetle is a bridge to the past, much the same as an old photo album: back to the euphoria felt at the creation of the Beetle, back to the time when it was misused as propaganda for the Nazis, back to the struggling beginning.

Driving for pleasure — Stuttgart 1956

Shadow of a world traveler. Times change, but the form stays the same: the Beetle — born in the country — at home on every continent.

Its curves mirror the passage of time; born in the shadow of dictatorship, the Beetle grew into a time when German practicality clashed with the elegance of kidney-shaped tables and bikinis. The fact that it has remained relatively the same over the years allows us to experience the Beetle as if we had been with it since the beginning. Even today, the Beetle is preparing for the turn of the century and its future, which should surprise no one: this car has incredible staying power. What is so exciting is that the sequel to the Beetle is being introduced 60 years after the car's premiere. The legend lives on, as you'll see in Chapter 8 of this book.

The Beetle takes us on a journey through time. This particular volume, however, shouldn't be interpreted as a record of every detail, every moment: rather, each picture should be able to stand on its own and evoke personal memories for the reader. The constant is always the car, as round and robust as Grandma Elisabeth.

A backward glance, full of melancholy —Rome 1965

This could almost be a scene from the Hitchcock thriller "The Birds." The story of the Beetle is like a Hollywood screenplay — full of ambition and drama. Even the finale is celebrated in the style of the old master, Alfred — hope for the future.

Memories are selective. You can't just scroll through your mind like it's a computer file. Each memory is a snapshot of a moment in time—the very personal moments of euphoria as well as those that are as sharp in our minds as the day they happened. The stories that are really worth retelling deal with the daily drama in our lives.

MOMENTS IN TIME

Why, for instance, is this man standing in his over-turned car while yelling at a policeman? All the officer had done was to motion the man to move into the far right lane on the highway because there was a construction site in the left lane 100 meters away. In the face of authority, the driver lost all common sense and turned the steering wheel too sharply to the right, cutting right in front of the truck he had been passing. With no other option, the truck rammed the Bug, which flipped twice and landed in the emergency lane. The man escaped without injury, even though he hadn't been wearing a seatbelt. The policeman, on the other hand, wasn't so lucky.

Stand By Me. The opportunities to stand up in your Beetle seem endless, whether it's a quiet moment on the beach or conflict on the roadside.

This is the life, relaxing on the beach on a sunny day with a companion and a perfect view of a brand-new baby blue Cabriolet. What more could anyone want?

In requisite hat and coat, the driver of the Beetle holds his course. The pedestrian walks by with nary a glance outside the protection of her umbrella, but the driver isn't any better off in his car—most Beetles at the time didn't come with a heating system as standard equipment.

For holidays and everyday. The three pairs of sunglasses peering through the oval rear window show something new for 1953: on March 10th, the charming split window disappeared and in its place appeared the oval. This change didn't tamper with the Beetle's status as the car for every task. In the photo below, for instance, the Beetle serves as a backdrop for the women selling vegetables at the open marketplace in Regensburg (Bavaria).

The grime of the city in the rain. In the mid '60s, the center of Stuttgart was still open to traffic. Three decades later, the quick turn the driver made onto Königsstraße would have ended in a pedestrian mall.

The mad rush to own a car had not yet begun as these Buessing trucks
make their way across Marienplatz in Munich (left). People were true
pedestrians and the sidewalks were wider than the streets, yet only a
few years later there wasn't a parking space to be had (above).

In 1965, the German Automobile Association (ADAC) recommended the use of the three-finger symbol to say "excuse me"(above, bottom). This gesture has disappeared along with uniformed gas station attendants, who even washed your windows and canvas tops (left). What has remained though and proliferated is the number of meter maids (above, top): Frankfurt has had them since 1961.

Ladies in Germany in the 1950s didn't go anywhere alone. Whether in Wolfsburg or elsewhere they always had a companion with them. If you didn't have a luxurious stroller with chrome fenders on hand (above), a loyal dachshund would do (left).

Mobility and immobility. Two
classic cars in a duel: a civilian
Beetle versus a Mercedes
police car (above)—and the
Beetle won.

This other Beetle (right) wasn't
so lucky. The driver barely
escaped injury: passersby
quickly pulled him from his car
as a streetcar fell on it.

With his hat in his hand, his eyes closed, this man has found his own parking spot—the quiet life in the center of Frankfurt, May 1963.

Happiness is holding hands. In 1964, wanderlust and the love of the car dominated the land.

A poll of Beetle owners in 1958 revealed sentiments such as: "To own a Beetle is to be in love." Many people called the Beetle "the first great love of their lives" (hopefully not the last!).

Simply decorated—the classless Beetle as a wedding carriage. The photographer noted that the festive narcissus arrangement at the base of the windshield cost five to seven Deutschmarks, probably the same price as the polish for the car.

"Babies are coming" was the watchword at Volkswagen of America as
they started the "Bonds for Babies Born in Beetles" campaign. There was
a small monetary reward given to mothers who gave birth in Beetles. Good
publicity, but inexpensive, as only 20 births a year occurred in Beetles.

Metamorphosis. Hans Kusche, an amateur mechanic, took a 1952 Beetle, shortened it substantially, removed the roof and *voilà!*—a roadster (top). His son is really enjoying himself, but his daughter looks a little skeptical.

To own a Beetle with a canvas sunroof was a future dream for the sons who wore shorts. In the meantime, they had to be content with being chauffeured down to the river by their father, who turned the trip into a Kodak moment (bottom).

Under the loving eye of his mother, a small boy enjoys his seat on the roof of a Beetle.

Happy as can be at first, children soon grew weary of the cramped quarters of the Beetle (above). Parents always hoped that sleep would overcome their tots, but kids in 1965 were no different from kids today— they will only fall asleep a block from home.

A portrait of a
Beetle—with five
extras (right). Film
and developing
was still a luxury
in 1952, so the
star of the family
is in the center,
with the rest on
the periphery.

37

This parade of cars represents a day's work at the Wolfsburg factory in the early 1950s. It is a parable of the German work ethic: one should be hardworking, orderly and always a little intimidating.

To today's German citizens, children of the Federal Republic of Germany, mass hysteria at the sight of the man with the small moustache, the screams of Sieg-Heil and miles of people with their arms raised seem so foreign. March 8, 1934 saw the first use of the Volkswagen as propaganda for the power-hungry Hitler. At the opening of the Berlin Auto Show, he proclaimed, "Today in Germany there is only one car for every 100 citizens. This must change."

TEMPTATION

The automobile was like a drug for the people who were thrilled with the thought of owning their own car, travelling all over the country on the soon-to-be built autobahns. The lie continued: Hitler maintained that the car wouldn't cost over 900 Reichsmarks and there would soon be over a million cars in Germany. Actually, it wasn't until 20 years later, on August 5, 1955, that total Beetle production crossed the million mark; and the price of this special jubilee car was DM 3790, the lowest Beetle price ever. Just before the currency reform of June 20, 1948, the price of a Volkswagen had been even higher at 5300 Reichsmarks. The "car for the people" never came to be under Hitler's rule. The Nazi leader had realized this as early as 1934, even as he was lifting the hopes of the German people.

The role of the Volkswagen has certainly changed over the last 60 years. Today, the Beetle allows us a unique view into Germany's past that we would otherwise never have.

A large crowd cheers as the cornerstone of the Volkswagen factory is laid in May 1938. The first look at the Beetle was awe-inspiring.

In 1937, to the leading automotive representatives of the time, the VW-30 Beetle prototype must have seemed too low to the ground, too round, and quite uncomfortable. During a stop for gas, Ferdinand Porsche stands quite sullen with his hands in his pockets and ignores the uncertain glances.

(The banner reads, "The first KdF-cars built at the Volkswagen factory, 1941.")
The first Volkswagen prototypes were presented with much pomp, even as Europe was in flames.
These cars, rather than being the later color of gray, were gleaming in black and chrome. This was
an attempt to reflect a sense of normality, in contrast with the abnormal headlight covers.

May 1938: 70,000 people came out to pay tribute to the new Beetle (above, top). As the Master of Ceremonies, Hitler stood behind the white block of granite that would be the corner-stone of the Volkswagen factory (above, bottom). This spectacle was a demonstration of the power of Nazi Germany. Approximately 150 journalists were on hand to report on this media extravaganza (of course, their reports were censored).

Hitler required that every KdF-Wagen (KdF stood for Kraft durch Freude, or "Strength through Joy"), as he dubbed the Beetle, hold at least four people. The press release at the time stated that parents and children should be able to travel together through the German countryside (right).

Construction of the Volkswagen factory began in 1938, at a site located approximately two kilometers from Wolfsburg Castle. Driving up to Klieversberg, a hill above Wolfsburg, afforded journalists a much better view of the scope of the project. They made the trip in prototype Beetles.

Using a miniature prototype, Ferdinand
Porsche describes the design of the Beetle
to his customers. A wooden crate,
addressed to the Führer and Reichskanzler
of greater Germany, Berlin, was used to
transport the model (above, top).

Months later, at the laying of the foundation
of the Volkswagen factory, Porsche
describes the many superior features of the
Beetle Cabriolet to Hitler. This time Porsche
uses a full-size pre-production prototype
(above, bottom).

(The License plate reads: "Test Vehicle")
The German army was on its last legs as Porsche visited
Prague in 1944. After the war, this self-educated Bohemian
collected a 1-DM licensing fee for every Beetle produced.

In 1937, SS soldiers covered over two
million kilometers as test drivers for
the VW-30 Series prototypes.

Filling up in 1936. The early Beetle with its mounted
headlights must have seemed futuristic compared
to the boxy shape of the BMW Dixi.

An ad campaign on wheels:
Large numbers of Volkswagens
traveled around the country.

Great publicity: At the Berlin
Auto Show in 1939, a Beetle
convoy rolls through the city.

Propaganda in the brochures of the time described the "car for the people" as a "miracle car." To own a Beetle was a dream come true: 336,668 people each saved 5 Reichsmarks per week for the opportunity to be one of the first to take delivery of a Beetle.

That the Kraft-durch-Freude ("Strength through Joy") car shouldn't cost more than a
motorcycle was the developers' mandate. The price had to be under 1000 Reichsmarks to
make this rendezvous under the sun possible.

Not long after the Beetle went into production, the idyllic world as presented in the pictures to the left existed only in the minds of advertisers.

Temporary solutions were the reality. As the war turned toward German soil and sources of oil dried up, Beetles and Kubelwagens were adapted to run on wood instead of gasoline.

The first six production cars appeared like a mirage in the desert. Until April 1945, the assembly line produced only Kubelwagens (bucket cars) and Schwimmwagens (swimming cars), a total of 66,000 cars. These models were the main focus of the factory, with only a handful of Beetles assembled, mostly in field gray (the color of German army uniforms).

Before it even had a chance, the Beetle seemed doomed. A massive bombing in 1945 destroyed 63% of the factory, yet only 630 civilian KdF-vehicles had been produced up to that point. That the Beetle survived even though the Nazis didn't is proof of the car's flexibility.

On May 25, 1945, the city of the KdF car was renamed Wolfsburg to signal its rebirth. The city was named after the nearby castle belonging to the Earl of Schulenburg. At the same time, the Volkswagen factory became (temporarily) the Wolfsburg Motor Works. Only at the urging of the citizens of Wolfsburg had the war in the city ceased on April 10. American forces stopped their march toward the city 10 kilometers to the west and did not occupy, at first, the future city of

RESURRECTION

Wolfsburg. The young city was an Allied bombing target because of its production of Kubelwagens, mines and grenade cases; but apparently was not a target for the ground forces. Because of fear of plundering by freed laborers, however, the town's religious leaders begged the Americans to occupy the factory and the city. The Americans stayed only a short while. After the partitioning of Germany into four zones, Wolfsburg came under British control.

In 1945, there were still 6,033 workers at the VW factory, while the city had a population of 17,109. The dream of a prospering auto metropolis lay in shambles. Major a.D (außer Dienst, meaning retired) Ivan Hirst, a member of the controlling commission in Germany, was one of the first to propose that the factory start up production again, even as most of the city still lay in ruin. Only 58 Beetles were produced in 1945, mostly by hand. But by March 1946, the 1000th Volkswagen Beetle rolled off the assembly line.

The people of Wolfsburg faced 1945 with little hope and few job prospects. Their only hope was something from their past—the Beetle (left).

Until the wall was built in 1962, you could still drive your Volkswagen from east to west. After that the road leading to the Brandenburg gate became a dead end (right: sign reads, "Warning!: You are leaving West Berlin in 40 meters").

Like the phoenix rising from the ashes, from the ruins comes rebirth. Shortly after almost total destruction, the Wolfsburg factory again began to produce Beetles. In 1953, Newsweek used this phenomenon to name the rebirth of the Volkswagen factory as Success Story Number One in postwar Germany.

A revolutionary sign of the times. By the end of 1945, the German name "Volkswagenwerk" (Volkswagen factory) had already returned, underneath the British designation "Wolfsburg Motor Works" (left, top). Most of the early postwar production went to the Allied Forces. Beetle bodies were attached to Kubelwagen frames to replenish the Allies' decimated stores (left, bottom).

The first day off for the factory was in March 1946 as the 1000th postwar Beetle rolled off the assembly line (below).

Return to normalcy. Press releases returned in 1947. The model holds her non-photogenic sunglasses demurely in her hand.

In 1947, the Volkswagen ads showed as much a lack of men as a lack of outside mirrors (below).

In a military lineup, the first all-terrain Beetles (Type 51) stand at attention in front of the bombed VW factory in 1945 (left).

Dire conditions breed unconventional solutions. The outlandish Beetles seen in the pictures are a sign of the times. Frames from all-terrain Beetles were paired with the appropriate body for the job. The top picture shows a mail truck pulling a small trailer (Type 83), while the middle picture is that of a Red Cross pickup truck (Type 92). A stretcher was placed all the way up to the windshield. The type 100 Beetle (bottom) takes its place in the VW history books as a tractor.

The first postwar Beetles emerged from the air raid shelter at the Volkswagen factory (right). This is where production was moved during the war.

(The banner reads, "The 2000th Volkswagen since the end of the war, January 1948.")
Light and shadow dominate this picture of a minor triumph. Like a Rembrandt master-
piece, the photograph captures the true atmosphere of the moment. Exhausted but
with hope for the future, the factory workers celebrate the rebirth of the factory.

Although Germany was no longer home to such a reality, pictures of the Volkswagen assembly lines within the massive factories still remind one of Fritz Lang's futuristic vision. Lang's 1927 film, "Metropolis," portrayed leaders in huge skyscrapers towering above the dark masses of workers. After a trip to America in 1937, Ferdinand Porsche brought back the newest machinery, including towering steel presses that stamped out sheet metal with their massive strength. Throughout

METROPOLIS

the floor of the factory, hundreds of kilometers of assembly lines were laid down to bring the innumerable parts of the Beetle together. Large cranes running along the roof of the factory ensured that the body and chassis of the car were precisely assembled.

Heinz Nordhoff came to the factory on January 1, 1948 and dramatically increased production efficiency. His goal was to reduce the number of hours required to assemble a Beetle from 400 to 100. Any mechanical device that could increase production was put to use. Whether this meant robots or conveyer belts, it didn't matter. "Complete tire and rim assemblies appear out of a hole in the earth," wrote a journalist of the time, reflecting the sense that the factory was like something out of a science fiction novel.

Overlooked by the uninitiated, every gear is connected to another, every machine blends into the next, every worker the same. Actual distinct faces do emerge, though, out of this anonymity. These are the thoughtful, introspective people, seen hard at work in the many photographs taken at the factory. Nordhoff's definition of the model Volkswagen employee comes to life in the workers' intense dedication and attention to detail.

The Beetle assembly line (left) seems to disappear into the vastness of the factory; the VW inspector (right), on the other hand, is quite close at hand.

The assembly-line workers follow the wooden assembly line as it moves forward in stages. Every 10 meters there is another worker with another task.

A two-man job: Workers had to be extra careful when removing a Beetle roof from the press. Hands and forearms were particularly vulnerable to cuts from the razor-sharp metal.

Two become one. The moment when the frame is attached to the body is referred to as the "wedding" in production lingo. This stage of the Beetle's construction seemed to get easier for the factory workers during the 1960s (top), but in actuality the basics were still the same. Since the beginning, though, there was a constant strive toward perfection (middle) reflected in constant improvements made to production. One such improvement, seen as early as 1949, was to use one central hook instead of four to carry the painted body across the factory.

A surreal light bathes Volkswagen factory workers as they assemble Beetle frames, while the shells they will be mated to seem to stand at attention.

With the precision of a surgeon, a factory worker readies a boxer motor for transport down the assembly line.

By the 1960s, more and more of the production process was automated. In 1952, however, Beetle shells were still manually pushed along the production line to the interior production area. This gave workers a chance for a quick chat.

The steel presses (right), their huge gears turning at lightning speed, dwarf the workers below.

Men's work. Women's work. Wearing a white lab coat, a young worker critically examines chrome hubcaps, 1956 (top). A solemn woman, her hair tightly pulled back, polishes steel rims, one after the other (bottom).

Using acetone and gasoline, four women give a car
its final polish: two work on the windows, two on the
finish. In 1954, Volkswagen gave women with
children an extra day off. It was called "wash day."

Four men are needed for the steel press.
Two place a hood into the machine, while two
others stand ready to take it out on the other
side and place it back on the assembly line.

Separation: women on the
left, men on the right. Men
and women still worked dis-
tinctly separated, as shown in
this 1962 photo of a seat production line. The attitudes
toward work at that time
were also very different.
There was a time for chat and
a time for work (above).

Assembly. A Beetle body is
carefully lowered onto the
chassis of a 1953 car (below).

The union. The separate parts
of these Beetles have traveled
hundreds of kilometers prior to
the "wedding," as seen here in
1961. In the next model year,
the Wolfsburg crest was
removed from the trunk lid.

Alone among the fenders. In
1957, there were seven colors
to choose from: prairie beige,
diamond green, polar silver,
horizon blue, black, coral red,
and agave green.

In 1957, over 1000 Beetle shells were on the move daily throughout the factory. In that model year, 32,634 workers produced 380,561 cars—one car every minute.

January 1978 was the end of an era, as the last German-built Beetle rolled off the assembly line. Yet there are still thousands of early Volkswagens on Germany's roads. This is a monument not only to the quality of the old-timer but to its long-standing popularity in the country of its birth.

MASS PRODUCTION

Although the Beetle was a monument to the economic marvel of Germany, it was hardly a car only for Germans. The Beetle was built in 20 countries and sold all over the world. America was the Beetle continent: while 9.7 million Beetles were sold in Europe, more than 10 million were sold from Alaska to Tierra del Fuego. Per-country sales show Germany clearly at the top with 8 million, but five million Beetles were sold in the USA and 3.5 million "Escarabajos" were sold in Mexico. The total number of Beetles produced reached 21,246,042 by March 1995. It is curious that, between the economic reforms of 1948 and later years, the price didn't continually rise. It started at DM 5300, went down to DM 4800 in 1949, dropped to DM 3950 in 1954, and then fell to DM 3790 at the celebration of the 1,000,00th Beetle in August 1955. This was the last time the Beetle's price dropped, however. Even at the end of Beetle production in Wolfsburg, January 1978, Volkswagen raised the price for the least-expensive Beetle by DM 80 to DM 7865. The last Beetle shipment from Mexico to Emden (Germany) took place seven years later. And that is the end to the story of the Beetle in Germany. Beetle production continues on in Mexico and beginning in August 1993, in Brazil as well, in the old "Fusca" factory, vacant for 9 years.

It's not a trick. It's a Volkswagen. Many of the five million Beetles imported into the U.S. landed at the port in Newark (New Jersey). Not all of them, however, were "hoisted" onto the dock by dock worker Joe Walker.

Through a relatively small door, a Beetle train rolls out of the factory in this 1956 photo. These cars are the standard German model, whereas the cars in the foreground await export to Canada, Guam and the United States.

In 1948, Beetles were still driven to the dealers in long processions by factory workers (above).

Ben Pon of Holland and his drivers were only able to take five cars with them as they took delivery of the first export Beetles (below, top). By 1950, Volkswagen used the then-modern Magirus car carriers to deliver cars to licensed dealers (below, bottom; right).

Even before the war, Ben Pon, a car dealer from Holland, had signed a
contract with Ferdinand Porsche to be the official importer of Volkswagens.
After the war, he was still involved with these small cars; but in January
1949, his attempt to become the US-importer of Volkswagens failed when
he ran out of money. The sample car he brought to New York did help him to
get home, though, after he sold it to a Swede for $800.

With the introduction of
the large canvas sunroof
in 1950, Beetle owners
could enjoy an unob-
structed view of the sky.
To enjoy their new Beetle
at its best, buyers always
opened the sunroof, even
in the strongest winds
(top). For extra fresh air,
even when the sunroof
was closed, this 1951
export vehicle came
equipped with air inlets
behind the front fenders.

Maneuvering this
1950 split-window
Beetle backwards up
a narrow ramp
required a very good
eye, especially with-
out a rearview mirror.

In the late 1940s, a few warehouses and train cars sufficed to hold Beetles ready for transport (only 86,182 Beetles were made between 1945 and 1949). 1950 saw a dramatic increase in output, with over 80,000 cars made.

By the middle of the 1960s, Volkswagen had over 80 ships at its disposal, which constituted the largest private charter fleet in the world. Emden became the world's most important automobile port.

The 100,000th Beetle. The first large-scale celebration at Wolfsburg took place on March 4, 1950. At the time, a standard Beetle cost DM 5,050, while an export sedan cost DM 5,700. The home market share for the Beetle at the time was an astounding 49.3%.

The Beetle's many attributes are legendary. "The Beetle will go anywhere," gushed a Volkswagen sales brochure. "The Beetle can run at top speed for hours from one horizon to the next," reads another poetic musing on this spartan marathon machine." The Beetle can handle any terrain, whether it be flat, hilly, crossing bridges, going through tunnels or cruising through the light pollution of a city." The all-season vehicle. As the advertisers were hyping their marathon runner from

ON THE ROAD

Germany, Ralph Nader's assessment was less than positive. Nader, who had become a consumer advocate, declared, "I don't think there is any other car out there that is as dangerous as the Volkswagen." Henceforth, he was considered an authority by many car safety experts. Two years later, the consequences of Nader's statement were astounding. Americans were buying 1300 Beetles a day and 1968 was a record year, with 423,000 Beetles sold in America. In the 1960s, the Beetle truly was a dangerous car—a threat to the Detroit automobile industry.

What brought the Beetle world renown were not the sales figures, but the Beetle's many feats. Anyone could just jump in a Beetle and drive over the Alps, across a desert, or even through a channel. Naturally, the first car in Antarctica was a Beetle.

The Beetle was everywhere. Morocco or Matterhorn—it didn't matter. This was a cosmopolitan car for which no trip was too long, no task too difficult.

"What the mule is for the gaucho, the four-cylinder Beetle is for the modern Mexican,"
read Volkswagen's ad for the first true world car. The Beetle fit in everywhere. It didn't
matter whether you were in Taxco (Mexico), in Texas or in Castrop Rauxel (Germany).

Four out of five new cars registered in Sao Paulo, Brazil in 1968 (right) were
Beetles. The yellow sand trails in Australia saw far fewer Volkswagens.
Occasionally, though, you encounter one (above), as seen in this 1994 photo.

Small talk in the Rockies.
The bear is either fascinated
by the new gas gauge in
this export Cabriolet or,
more likely, by the equally
fascinated woman in the
passenger seat.

The last inhabitant of the
hermitage at San Colombano
in Vallarsa, Italy died in 1766.
However, pilgrims still make
the climb to this holy place
built in 650 (left). Because of
the constant drought-like
conditions, the pilgrims pray
to the holy Colombano for
rain. Of course, there is a
Beetle present.

Cargo ship investors were
ferried close to the Silvretta
alpine road near the
Schneeglocke.

First impressions are
deceiving. The Beetle
really doesn't need its own
tent, even near the salt
water of the North Sea.

The "Speed Limit 100 km/h" sign is a joke—
June 29, 1968 was a bad day to be on the road.
Summer vacations and the resulting autobahn
chaos began simultaneously in Holland, Belgium,
North Rhine-Westfalia (Germany), and Sweden.

Wherever the road leads. In 1964, Franz Kuehn and Bernd Schlesinger crossed the Strait of Messina in a Beetle. Twenty years later, their Beetle was on the water again: this time on Starnberg Lake, floating on an inflatable raft.

No parking space is too small.
This is an example of one of
the many ad campaigns with
which Volkswagen extolled the
virtues of the Beetle (above).
The ad reads, "The Beetle is
small, imported and only has a
small amount of chrome trim.
Why, then, is this car the fourth
most popular in America?"

This 1963 Beetle
(right) traveled over
2000 kilometers on
alpine roads all the
way up to the blocked
Albula Pass. Gas
mileage: 29.5 miles
per gallon (7.6 liters
per 100 kilometers).

3000 kilometers from Tuxtla Gutierrez to the Rio Grande. At the Carrera Panamerica, Mexico's legendary road race, Germany's original car for the masses challenges the American behemoths: four cylinders vs. massive V8s.

Three photos of countries where Beetles truly made it. Over 17 million Volkswagens were sold in the United States, Germany and Mexico combined.

The shadows of two export Beetles reflect off the snow near Denver, Colorado (left).

Above, two kids run up the steps of the Cathedral at Königslutter. The curves of the Beetle contrast sharply with the sharp angle of this Mayan pyramid on the Yucatán Peninsula (right).

Picasso supposedly used two toy Beetles as the head of a baboon sculpture.
Sculptor Eric Staller took an entire car, installed 1,659 light bulbs on it, and
put a generator in the trunk. His name for the car was "Manhattan."

Top-heavy. The shape of the Beetle is like that of an egg, the beginning of all life. Carrying bulky items on the roof seems as natural to the Beetle as the traditional methods of transporting goods seen in this photo (right) taken on a dusty road in East Africa.

Melancholy and wanderlust meet on the horizon. Balmy air sweeps across a serpentine road leading toward Bad Tölz as this Beetle from Munich comes to a halt next to a mile marker. A picture is worth a thousand words.

Heinz Nordhoff won the Elmar A. Sperry Award in 1958: standing next to Nordhoff in New York's Brass Rail restaurant was none other than Ferry Porsche. His father's creation, the Beetle, was recognized as outstanding in the automotive industry: the first time that a product of foreign soil was honored with the Sperry Award for outstanding industrial achievement. But the charming, independent lines of the Beetle weren't the focus of the award: rather, it was the fact that this compact car was developed with easy maintenance and adequate performance. This praise is almost an insult.

TRUE TO FORM

"As practical as a Tupperware container," was the phrase used by the judges of this car "made in Western Germany," proving that they had no real vision. Yes, the Beetle's intelligent, straight-forward construction was one of the factors leading to its success, but not the most important. It was the unique shape of the Beetle that drove people to buy the cars and cherish them. The provocative strategy developed in Wolfsburg was that the shape of the Beetle was progressive and modern, because the form was timeless—as timeless as a pencil, as perfect a form as a violin or an egg—a daring assertion, considering that the car was developed back in the early 1930s. Ferdinand Porsche developed the first prototype resembling the Beetle as early as 1932 for Zündapp. Just a year later, Porsche's prototype, developed under contract with NSU, more closely resembled the production Beetle. In 1994, Volkswagen definitively demonstrated the timelessness and modernity of the Beetle form when they introduced Concept 1, the Beetle for the year 2000. This new Beetle is most definitely a candidate for future design awards.

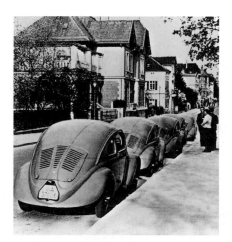

Evolution. From the prototype VW 30 lacking a rear window (left) to the Beetle with a rearward view (right).

You could climb into this 1934 NSU prototype (Code name: Type 32) wearing your hat. This forerunner of the Beetle never went into production but its close resemblance to the Beetle is obvious when they are side by side, as seen in this unique postwar photo.

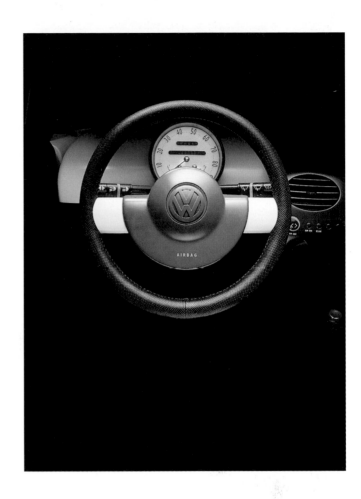

While common sense dictated the earlier styling of the Beetle, the Concept 1 was designed with true form in mind. The round, modern steering wheel with airbag encircles the centrally located speedometer. Both are cleanly integrated into the rounded dashboard.

Borrowing the
curved shape of
the Beetle, the
Concept 1 is a
true grandchild of
the original. It
debuted at the
1994 Detroit
Auto Show and
demonstrates
many similarities
with its ancestor.

The high point of design. The fashionable ambience of the 1994 Geneva Auto Show was the backdrop to the introduction of the Concept 1 Cabriolet (above). Even more elegant than the sedan, the Cabriolet bridges the gap between yesterday and today.

As time goes by. Volkswagen's reincarnation of a legend and its infamous ancestor. The modern version of the Karmann-built Cabriolet could be an authentic sequel to the original: the beginning of a wonderful, new friendship.

To squeeze 60 years of history into 144 pages isn't an easy task. Each reader will have unique reactions to the photographs here—long forgotten times will rise to the surface, children will remember the good times of their childhood. For those whose interest has been awakened after perusing the pictures in this book, there is a huge array of other interesting volumes from which to choose.

REFLECTION

The Beetle is a child of the streets, living in the driveways of ordinary people. Snobs drive the car only as long as it is fashionable. True enthusiasts are those people that value the Beetle's independent character and its eternally unique shape.

Trying to figure out why the Beetle became a world phenomenon, in spite of its failed beginning as the KdF-Wagen, is as useless as trying to understand the human fascination with the ocean. Whomever feels the pull, understands. It is impossible to explain in words.

Automotive Books From Robert Bentley

ENTHUSIAST BOOKS

Small Wonder: The Amazing Story of the Volkswagen Beetle *Walter Henry Nelson*
ISBN 0-8376-0147-9

Going Faster! Mastering the Art of Race Driving: The Skip Barber Racing School
Carl Lopez ISBN 0-8376-0227-0

The Racing Driver *Denis Jenkinson*
ISBN 0-8376-0201-7

Sports Car and Competition Driving *Paul Frère with foreword by Phil Hill*
ISBN 0-8376-0202-5

The Technique of Motor Racing *Piero Taruffi with foreword by Juan Manuel Fangio*
ISBN 0-8376-0228-9

Race Car Aerodynamics *Joseph Katz*
ISBN 0-8376-0142-8

Think To Win *Don Alexander with foreword by Mark Martin*ISBN 0-8376-0070-7

The Design and Tuning of Competition Engines *Philip H. Smith, 6th edition revised by David N. Wenner* ISBN 0-8376-0140-1

New Directions in Suspension Design: Making the Fast Car Faster *Colin Campbell*
ISBN 0-8376-0150-9

Maximum Boost: Designing, Testing, and Installing Turbocharger Systems *Corky Bell*
ISBN 0-8376-0160-6

Volkswagen Sport Tuning for Street and Competition *Per Schroeder*
ISBN 0-8376-0161-4

Harley-Davidson Evolution V-Twin Owner's Bible™ *Moses Ludel*
ISBN 0-8376-0146-0

Jeep Owner's Bible™ *Moses Ludel*
ISBN 0-8376-0154-1

Ford F-Series Pickup Owner's Bible™
Moses Ludel ISBN 0-8376-0152-5

Chevrolet & GMC Light Truck Owner's Bible™ *Moses Ludel*
ISBN 0-8376-0157-6

Toyota Truck & Land Cruiser Owner's Bible™ *Moses Ludel*
ISBN 0-8376-0159-2

Chevrolet by the Numbers™: 1955-1959
Alan Colvin ISBN 0-8376-0875-9

Chevrolet by the Numbers™: 1960-1964
Alan Colvin ISBN 0-8376-0936-4

Chevrolet by the Numbers™: 1965-1969
Alan Colvin ISBN 0-8376-0956-9

Chevrolet by the Numbers™: 1970-1975
Alan Colvin ISBN 0-8376-0927-5

Alfa Romeo Owner's Bible™
Pat Braden with foreword by Don Black
ISBN 0-8376-0707-9

The Scientific Design of Exhaust and Intake Systems *Philip H. Smith and John C. Morrison*
ISBN 0-8376-0309-9**The BMW Enthusiast's Companion** *BMW Car Club of America* ISBN 0-8376-0321-8

FUEL INJECTION

Ford Fuel Injection and Electronic Engine Control: 1988-1993 *Charles O. Probst, SAE*
ISBN 0-8376-0301-3

Ford Fuel Injection and Electronic Engine Control: 1980-1987 *Charles O. Probst, SAE*
ISBN 0-8376-0302-1

Bosch Fuel Injection and Engine Management *Charles O. Probst, SAE*
ISBN 0-8376-0300-5

VOLKSWAGEN OFFICIAL SERVICE MANUALS

Jetta, Golf, GTI, Cabrio Service Manual: 1993-1997, including Jetta$_{III}$ and Golf$_{III}$
Robert Bentley ISBN 0-8376-0365-X

GTI, Golf, and Jetta Service Manual: 1985-1992 Gasoline, Diesel, and Turbo Diesel, including 16V *Robert Bentley*
ISBN 0-8376-0342-0

Corrado Official Factory Repair Manual: 1990-1994 *Volkswagen United States*
ISBN 0-8376-0387-0

Passat Official Factory Repair Manual: 1990-1993, including Wagon *Volkswagen United States* ISBN 0-8376-0378-1

Cabriolet and Scirocco Service Manual: 1985-1993, including 16V *Robert Bentley*
ISBN 0-8376-0362-5

Volkswagen Fox Service Manual: 1987-1993, including GL, GL Sport and Wagon
Robert Bentley ISBN 0-8376-0340-4

Vanagon Official Factory Repair Manual: 1980-1991 including Diesel Engine, Syncro, and Camper *Volkswagen United States*
ISBN 0-8376-0336-6

Rabbit, Scirocco, Jetta Service Manual: 1980-1984 Gasoline Models, including Pickup Truck, Convertible, and GTI *Robert Bentley* ISBN 0-8376-0183-5

Rabbit, Jetta Service Manual: 1977-1984 Diesel Models, including Pickup Truck and Turbo Diesel *Robert Bentley*
ISBN 0-8376-0184-3

Rabbit, Scirocco Service Manual: 1975-1979 Gasoline Models *Robert Bentley*
ISBN 0-8376-0107-X

Dasher Service Manual: 1974-1981 including Diesel *Robert Bentley*
ISBN 0-8376-0083-9

Super Beetle, Beetle and Karmann Ghia Official Service Manual Type 1: 1970-1979
Volkswagen United States ISBN 0-8376-0096-0

Beetle and Karmann Ghia Official Service Manual Type 1: 1966-1969 *Volkswagen United States* ISBN 0-8376-0416-8

Station Wagon/Bus Official Service Manual Type 2: 1968-1979 *Volkswagen United States* ISBN 0-8376-0094-4

Fastback and Squareback Official Service Manual Type 3: 1968-1973 *Volkswagen United States* ISBN 0-8376-0057-X

AUDI OFFICIAL SERVICE MANUALS

Audi 100, A6 Official Factory Repair Manual: 1992-1997, including S4, S6, quattro and Wagon models. *Audi of America.*
ISBN 0-8376-0374-9

Audi 80, 90, Coupe Quattro Official Factory Repair Manual: 1988-1992 including 80 Quattro, 90 Quattro and 20-valve models
Audi of America ISBN 0-8376-0367-6

Audi 100, 200 Official Factory Repair Manual: 1988-1991 *Audi of America* ISBN 0-8376-0372-2

Audi 5000S, 5000CS Official Factory Repair Manual: 1984-1988 Gasoline, Turbo, and Turbo Diesel, including Wagon and Quattro *Audi of America* ISBN 0-8376-0370-6

Audi 4000S, 4000CS, and Coupe GT Official Factory Repair Manual: 1984-1987 including Quattro and Quattro Turbo *Audi of America* ISBN 0-8376-0373-0

BMW SERVICE MANUALS

BMW 5-Series Service Manual: 1982-1988 528e, 533i, 535i, 535is *Robert Bentley*
ISBN 0-8376-0318-8

BMW 3-Series Service Manual: 1984-1990 318i, 325, 325e(es), 325i(is), and 325i Convertible
Robert Bentley ISBN 0-8376-0325-0

SAAB OFFICIAL SERVICE MANUALS

Saab 900 16 Valve Official Service Manual: 1985-1993 *Robert Bentley* ISBN 0-8376-0312-9

Saab 900 8 Valve Official Service Manual: 1981-1988 *Robert Bentley* ISBN 0-8376-0310-2

Robert Bentley has published service manuals and automobile books since 1950. Please write Robert Bentley, Inc., Publishers, at 1734 Massachusetts Avenue, Cambridge, MA 02138, visit our web site at http://www.rb.com, or call 1800-423-4595 for a free copy of our complete catalog, including titles and service manuals for **Jaguar, Triumph, Austin-Healey, MG, Volvo**, and other cars.

Project #12,
or Type 12
(Zündapp Volksauto)

V1series
(Type 60, "V" for
Versuch, or Experiment):
2-door sedan

V3 series: all-steel
floor, 4-cylinder
"flat-four" engine

Additional VW30 series
prototype for 1938 added
split rear window
and running boards

VW62, evolved into VW82
or Kübelwagen (bucket car):
military vehicle, 1940-1945

Type 11 B
(same as
KdF-wage
painted m
military gr

1932   1933   1934   1935   1936   1937   1938   1939   1940   1941   1942   1943   1944   1945

V2 series:
convertible
(same as V1)

VW39 series, identical
in specification to VW38

VW38 series
(KdF-wagen)

Project #32,
or Type 32
(NSU, air-cooled
1.5-liter engine)

Schwimmwagen:
4-wheel drive
amphibian,
military vehicle,
1940-1945

VW30
series
prototype

Super Beetle introduced,
with MacPherson struts,
front disc brakes, and
luggage space doubled

Wolfsburg crest
eliminated

VW 1500 with
1.5-liter, 44-hp engine
and 12-volt electrical
system introduced

Door handles switched
from pull-out lever to grab-
handles with push-buttons

Double-jointed
rear axle introduced

Baja Champion S
(Super Beetle)
introduced; Baja
made available

1960   1961   1962   1963   1964   1965   1966   1967   1968   1969   1970   1971   1972   1973

Fuel tap
replaced
by gas
gauge

VW 1300
with 1.3-liter, 40-hp
engine introduced

Increased
horsepower
from 36 hp
to 40 hp

Pillars slimmer,
windows enlarged

Dual-port
1584-cc
engine,
60 hp

Single port
1584-cc
engine,
57 hp

Sport
(VW 1
packag
introdu
black t
and sp
front s
1.6-lite

Back window enlarged
in convertible; steel
sunroof introduced

Bumpers raised
and strengthened;
added safety
steering column